GRADE 3

240 Vocabulary Words Kids Need to Know

*24 Ready-to-Reproduce Packets
That Make
Vocabulary Building
Fun & Effective*

by Linda Ward Beech

SCHOLASTIC
Teaching
Resources

New York • Toronto • London • Auckland • Sydney
Mexico City • New Delhi • Hong Kong • Buenos Aires

Cover design by Gerard Fuchs

Interior design by Melinda Belter

Interior illustrations by Steve Cox, Mike Moran

ISBN: 0-439-28043-5

3 4 5 6 7 8 9 10   40   09 08 07 06 05 04 03

GRADE 3 Table of Contents

Using the Book

Where would we be without words? It's hard to imagine. Words are a basic building block of communication, and a strong vocabulary is an essential part of reading, writing, and speaking well. The purpose of this book is to help learners expand the number of words they know and the ways in which they use them. Although 240 vocabulary words are introduced, many more words and meanings are woven into the book's 24 lessons.

Learning new words is not just about encountering them; it's about using, exploring, and thinking about them. So the lessons in this book are organized around different aspects and attributes of words—related meanings, how words are formed, where words come from, coined words, homophones, homographs, word parts, clips, and much more. The lessons provide an opportunity for students to try out words and to reflect and have fun with them.

Materials: As you introduce the lessons, be sure to have the following items available:

> **dictionaries**
> **thesauruses**
> **writing notebooks or journals**
> **writing tools**

TIP You'll find a complete alphabetized list of all the lesson words at the back of the book.

Lesson Organization: Each lesson is three pages long and introduces ten words.

The first lesson page includes:

lesson words

statement of lesson focus

simple sentences explaining the meanings of the words

two exercises

The second page includes:

lesson words

cloze activity

thinking activity with test prep fill-ins

Writing to Learn component

The third page includes:

puzzle, game, or other learning activity using the words

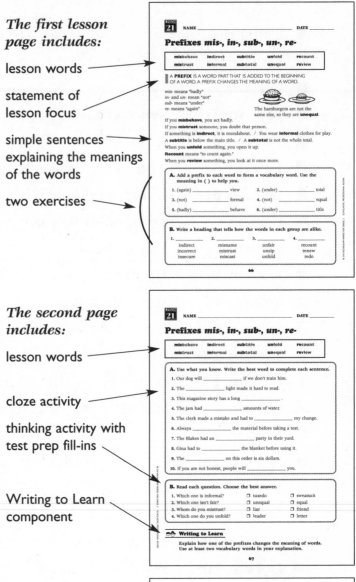

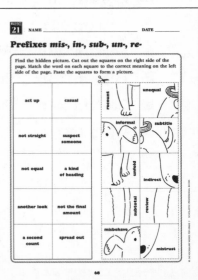

Tips for Using the Lessons

- Many words have more than one meaning, including some that are not given in the lesson. You may want to point out additional meanings or invite students to discover them independently.

- Many words can be used as more than one part of speech. Again, you can expand students' vocabulary by drawing attention to such usage.

- Have students complete the Writing to Learn activities in a notebook or journal so they have a specific place where they can refer to and review words.

- Consider having students make a set of word cards for each lesson, or make a class set and place it in your writing center.

- Don't hesitate to add your own writing assignments. The more students use a word, the more likely they are to "own" it.

- Be aware of pronunciation differences when teaching homographs. Not all students may pronounce words in the same way, and this can lead to confusion.

- Use the vocabulary words to teach related spelling and grammar rules.

- Encourage students to make semantic maps for some words. For instance, they might organize a map for a noun to show what the word is, what it is like, what it is not like, and include examples of the word.

- Have students illustrate some words.

- Help students make connections by pointing out lesson words used in other contexts and materials.

- Talk about other forms of a word, for example *loyal, loyalty, disloyal, loyalist*. Encourage students to word build in this fashion.

- Have students categorize words.

- Encourage students to consult more than one reference and to compare information.

> **TIP** Consider having students fill out Word Inventory Sheets before each lesson. The headings for such a sheet might be: Words I Know; Words I Have Seen but Don't Really Know; New Words. Using pencils, students can list the vocabulary words and probable meanings under the headings. As the lesson proceeds, they can make revisions and additions.

Synonyms

foe	purchase	absent	feeble	sturdy
vast	drowsy	prank	annual	reply

▎A **SYNONYM** IS A WORD THAT MEANS THE SAME
OR ALMOST THE SAME AS ANOTHER WORD.

When you **purchase** something, you buy it.

A **foe** is an enemy. / If something is **vast**, it is huge.
Drowsy means the same as sleepy.
If you are **absent**, you are missing.
A **prank** is a trick. / If you are **feeble**, you are weak.
An **annual** event is a yearly one.
If something is **sturdy**, it is strong. / A **reply** is an answer.

A. Read the word in the first column. Find and circle two other words
that mean almost the same thing

1. **prank**	joke	parade	trick
2. **foe**	friend	enemy	opponent
3. **reply**	answer	request	respond
4. **feeble**	foolish	weak	frail
5. **drowsy**	sleepy	drippy	tired
6. **sturdy**	weak	strong	tough
7. **vast**	huge	enormous	short

B. Cross out the word in each box that does not belong.

1.	gone	absent	missing	here
2.	buy	get	dunk	purchase

Synonyms

foe	purchase	absent	feeble	sturdy
vast	drowsy	prank	annual	reply

A. Use what you know. Write the best word to complete each sentence.

1. Once a year, Sara has an _____ checkup.

2. It costs ten dollars to _____ a ticket.

3. Seth did not _____ to the question.

4. The _____ table could hold the heavy plant.

5. The teacher has a cold and will be _____ today.

6. The opposite of a friend is a _____ .

7. The newborn bird was too _____ to fly.

8. Ron plans to play a _____ on his sister.

9. The _____ mall was the largest one Arooba had even seen.

10. The kitten grew _____ and soon fell asleep.

B. Read each question. Choose the best answer.

1. Who will make a purchase? ❑ seller ❑ buyer
2. Who will help you? ❑ pal ❑ foe
3. What do you call a missing person? ❑ present ❑ absent
4. Which one is an annual event? ❑ birthday ❑ breakfast

 Writing to Learn

Write a note to a friend. Use at least two of the vocabulary words.

NAME _____ DATE _____

Synonyms

Write a synonym for each word on the list. Then use the synonyms to help you trace a path through the maze.

1. answer _____

2. weak _____

3. sleepy _____

4. enemy _____

5. yearly _____

6. buy _____

7. missing _____

8. trick _____

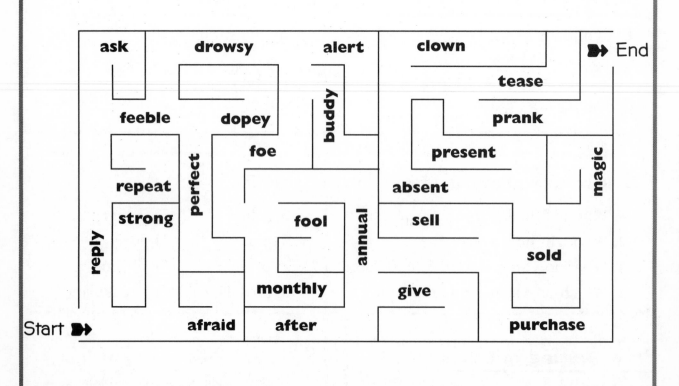

© 240 VOCABULARY WORDS FOR GRADE 3   SCHOLASTIC PROFESSIONAL BOOKS

Synonyms

shiver	slumber	banner	ill	stalk
voyage	meadow	loyal	vacant	wild

▌ A **SYNONYM** IS A WORD THAT MEANS THE SAME OR ALMOST THE SAME AS ANOTHER WORD.

A **voyage** is a trip.

When you **slumber**, you sleep.

A **meadow** is a field.

A **banner** is a flag.

If you are **loyal**, you are faithful.

If you are **ill**, you are sick.

If something is **vacant**, it is empty.

A **stalk** is a stem.

A **wild** animal is an untamed one.

A **shiver** is a shudder.

A. Read the word in the first column. Draw a line to match it with a synonym in the second column.

1. shiver   **a.** journey

2. meadow   **b.** sick

3. loyal   **c.** pasture

4. voyage   **d.** empty

5. slumber   **e.** devoted

6. ill   **f.** shake

7. vacant   **g.** snooze

B. Write a vocabulary word for each picture.

1.  _____

2.  _____

3.  _____

NAME _____ DATE _____

Synonyms

shiver	slumber	banner	ill	stalk
voyage	meadow	loyal	vacant	wild

A. Use what you know. Write the best word to complete each sentence.

1. The cold wind made Marly _____ .

2. Look! The _____ geese are flying south.

3. The passengers are eager to start their _____ .

4. A bright _____ hung on the wall.

5. In winter, a bear is deep in _____ .

6. Our school is _____ to its team.

7. That flower has a long _____ .

8. A flock of sheep grazed in the _____ .

9. Luke was _____ with the flu.

10. The abandoned motel was _____ .

B. Read each question. Choose the best answer.

1. What is a grassland? ❑ lawn ❑ meadow
2. Which one is a stalk? ❑ celery ❑ lettuce
3. Who takes a voyage? ❑ traveler ❑ treasurer
4. What might make you shiver? ❑ joke ❑ fear

✒ Writing to Learn

Pretend you are on a trip. Write a postcard to your family. Use at least two of the vocabulary words.

Synonyms

Read each pair of words. Draw a banner around them if they are
synonyms. Write a synonym if the pairs do *not* mean the same thing.

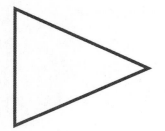

1.
stem
stalk
_____

2.
doze
slumber
_____

3.
loyal
unfaithful
_____

4.
wild
untamed
_____

5.
shudder
shiver
_____

6.
banner
balloon
_____

7.
meadow
field
_____

8.
voyage
vacation
_____

9.
vacant
full
_____

10.
ill
healthy
_____

Synonyms

slosh	**overcast**	**furious**	**task**	**orbit**
frayed	**mammoth**	**assist**	**lurk**	**bothersome**

A **SYNONYM** IS A WORD THAT MEANS THE SAME OR ALMOST THE SAME AS ANOTHER WORD.

When you splash, you **slosh**.

A worn cuff is a **frayed** one.

A cloudy day is **overcast**.

Something very large is **mammoth**.

If you are really angry, you are **furious**.

When you help people, you **assist** them. / A **task** is a job.

When you **lurk**, you wait. / If you circle Earth, you **orbit** it.

A **bothersome** noise is squeaky chalk!

A. Write your best idea for a synonym for each word. Then check your ideas in a dictionary or thesaurus.

1. slosh _____   2. assist _____

3. frayed _____   4. task _____

5. overcast _____   6. lurk _____

7. mammoth _____   8. orbit _____

B. Read each vocabulary word. Circle two other words that mean the same thing.

1. **furious**   upset   content   mad

2. **bothersome**   helpful   annoying   difficult

© 240 VOCABULARY WORDS FOR GRADE 3   SCHOLASTIC PROFESSIONAL BOOKS

NAME _____ DATE _____

Synonyms

slosh	overcast	furious	task	orbit
frayed	mammoth	assist	lurk	bothersome

A. Use what you know. Write the best word to complete each sentence.

1. Taking out the garbage was John's daily _____ .

2. The spaceship will _____ one more time before landing.

3. His coat was old and _____ at the collar.

4. Let's _____ through the puddles.

5. It is _____ when you tap your fingers like that.

6. The sky was dark and _____ without the sun.

7. The dent in her car made Alice _____ .

8. The tall building seemed _____ to the small boy.

9. My cat will _____ at her dish until I feed her.

B. Read the words in each row. Then write a vocabulary word that is a synonym.

1. huge, large, enormous _____

2. work, assignment, job _____

3. slop, splash, stir _____

4. help, aid, support _____

 Writing to Learn

Write a weather report. Use at least two of the vocabulary words.

Synonyms

Complete the puzzle. Find the synonym for each word.

Synonyms Across

2. angry
4. worn
5. job
8. cloudy
9. annoying
10. help

Synonyms Down

1. wait
3. circle
6. splash
7. large

Antonyms

deep	flexible	pain	repair	infant
shallow	rigid	pleasure	break	adult

▌AN **ANTONYM** IS A WORD THAT MEANS
THE OPPOSITE OF ANOTHER WORD.

When you **break** something, glue can **repair** it.

A **deep** pool has many feet of water, but a **shallow** pool does not.

Something **flexible** bends easily, and something **rigid** is very stiff.

You feel **pain** when something bad happens and **pleasure** when something good happens.

If you **break** something, you need to **repair** or fix it.

An **infant** is a baby, and an **adult** is a grownup.

A. Read the word in the first column. Find and circle the word that has the opposite meaning.

1. **pain**	hurt	joy	silly
2. **repair**	destroy	fix	review
3. **infant**	babe	teen	grownup
4. **shallow**	shadow	deep	cover
5. **break**	shatter	restore	crack
6. **rigid**	stiff	flexible	unbending

B. Write a vocabulary word that is the opposite of each picture.

1.  _____

2. _____

3. _____

Antonyms

deep	flexible	pain	repair	infant
shallow	rigid	pleasure	break	adult

A. Use what you know. Write the best word to complete each sentence.

1. The cradle was the right size for the _____ .

2. When there's no rain, the river becomes _____ .

3. Winning gives a team a great deal of _____ .

4. A ticket for an _____ costs more than one for a child.

5. Dad will _____ the loose shutter.

6. The water in the well is from _____ in the ground.

7. When the clay hardened, it was very _____ .

8. If you drop that glass, it will surely _____ .

9. The _____ material could bend easily.

10. Sue was in _____ after she twisted her ankle.

B. Read each question. Choose the best answer.

1. Which one is bigger?   ❑ adult   ❑ infant
2. Which one is better?   ❑ pain   ❑ pleasure
3. Which end of the pool is for wading?   ❑ deep   ❑ shallow
4. What is glue best for?   ❑ repair   ❑ break

Writing to Learn

Write an ad for a baby toy. Use at least two of the vocabulary words.

Antonyms

Rewrite Mark's note to his grandmother. Use an antonym for each underlined word.

Dear Nana,

We had four feet of snow this week! Some of the drifts are really <u>shallow</u>. Dad is going to <u>break</u> my sled so I can ride down the hill on it. Mom says the snow is more of a <u>pain</u> for me than for her. That's because an <u>infant</u> has to worry about driving on slippery roads.

Come see us soon.

Mark

_____

_____

_____

_____

_____

_____

NAME _____   DATE _____

Antonyms

bright	tidy	attic	borrow	gracious
dim	sloppy	cellar	lend	rude

▎AN **ANTONYM** IS A WORD THAT MEANS
THE OPPOSITE OF ANOTHER WORD.

If the light is too **bright**, you can turn it down and make it **dim**.

A tidy room is **neat**, and a **sloppy** room is messy.

An **attic** is at the top of a house, and a **cellar** is at the bottom.

When you **borrow**, you get something. When you **lend**,
you give something.

A **gracious** person is polite. A **rude** person is not polite.

A. Read the word in the first
column. Draw a line to
match it with an antonym in
the second column.

1. **bright**   **a.** basement

2. **tidy**   **b.** rude

3. **gracious** **c.** share

4. **attic**   **d.** dull

5. **borrow** **e.** untidy

B. Use a colored pencil to shade
the two boxes with antonyms
in each rectangle.

1.

lend	lone
borrow	own

2.

salt	buyer
loft	cellar

3.

tide	sloppy
slippery	orderly

Antonyms

bright	tidy	attic	borrow	gracious
dim	sloppy	cellar	lend	rude

A. Use what you know. Write the best word to complete each sentence.

1. The builders dug a hole for the _____ of the house.

2. Our cat is very _____ and never spills a drop of milk.

3. On July days, the sun is very _____ .

4. Liam treated all his friends at the party in a _____ manner.

5. Clothes and toys were thrown everywhere in the _____ room.

6. Fred needs to _____ a sleeping bag for the camping trip.

7. We couldn't see well in the _____ light.

8. Let's see what's in the old trunk up in the _____ .

9. Malik felt it was _____ of Theo not to shake hands.

10. If you're chilly, Jane will _____ you a sweater.

B. Read each question. Choose the best answer.

1. Which one is downstairs? ❏ attic ❏ cellar
2. Who is sloppy? ❏ slob ❏ soldier
3. Which light is best for a nap? ❏ bright ❏ dim
4. How can you get money? ❏ lend ❏ borrow

Writing to Learn

You find a box of old treasures. Write a description of your discovery.
Use at least two vocabulary words.

Antonyms

Play Tic-Tac-Antonym. Read each word. Then draw a line through three words in the box that are antonyms for that word. Your line can be vertical, horizontal, or diagonal.

1. tidy

messy	sloppy	disorderly
tile	neat	late
shirt	tie	tired

2. dim

dull	den	shiny
sweet	heavy	brilliant
cloud	night	bright

3. lend

land	money	obtain
send	borrow	give
receive	need	release

4. bright

broad	faint	lamp
smart	dim	morning
bulb	dark	starry

5. sloppy

slosh	drippy	slobber
clean	perfect	slow
neat	orderly	tidy

NAME _____ DATE _____

Compound Words

eyelid	waterfall	lunchtime	springboard	rainbow
birdbath	keyboard	hairbrush	scorekeeper	catfish

■ A **COMPOUND WORD** IS MADE UP OF TWO
SMALLER WORDS PUT TOGETHER.

It's a bath for birds.   It's a birdbath!

An **eyelid** protects your eye.

When a river drops over a cliff, it creates a **waterfall**.

A piano has a **keyboard** that you play.

The middle meal of the day is **lunchtime**.

You use a **hairbrush** to brush your hair.

A **springboard** is a flexible board you jump from.

A **scorekeeper** keeps the score during a game.

A **rainbow** is a band of colors. / A **catfish** is a fish with whiskers.

A. Complete each sentence with a vocabulary word.

1. A brush for your hair is a _____ .

2. A fish that looks like a cat is a _____ .

3. A lid that covers an eye is an _____ .

4. When it is time for lunch, it is _____ .

5. A bath for a bird is a _____ .

B. Write the two words that make up each compound word.

1. waterfall   **2. rainbow**   **3. keyboard**

_____ + _____   _____ + _____   _____ + _____

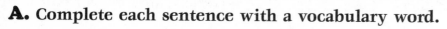

       4. springboard   **5. scorekeeper**

       _____ + _____   _____ + _____

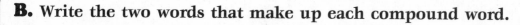

Compound Words

eyelid	waterfall	lunchtime	springboard	rainbow
birdbath	keyboard	hairbrush	scorekeeper	catfish

A. Use what you know. Write the best word to complete each sentence.

1. The musician's hands moved over the _____ .

2. A robin sat on the _____ , looking at the water.

3. She closed one _____ and winked.

4. A colorful _____ appeared after the storm.

5. Jeb was very hungry at _____ .

6. Sally put her comb and _____ on the dresser.

7. In the third inning, the _____ recorded three hits for our team.

8. A _____ is good to eat if you can catch it.

9. It isn't safe to swim near the top of a _____ .

10. The gymnast pushed off the _____ at the end of the event.

B. Read each question. Choose the best answer.

1. Which one swims? ❑ catnap ❑ catfish
2. When do you eat? ❑ lunchtime ❑ overtime
3. Which one makes music? ❑ keyboard ❑ keyhole
4. Which one shuts? ❑ eyelash ❑ eyelid

✎ **Writing to Learn**

Choose two vocabulary words. Write a riddle for each.

Compound Words

Write a word for each picture. Then write the compound word.

1.    +   = _____

2.    +   = _____

3.   +   = _____

4.    +   = _____

5.   +   = _____

6.    +   = _____

7. **lunch**   +   = _____

8.   +   **fall**   = _____

Compound Words

beehive	**hillside**	**applesauce**	**crosswalk**	**railroad**
sandbox	**spaceship**	**homework**	**turtleneck**	**rowboat**

▌ A **COMPOUND WORD** IS MADE UP OF TWO
▌ SMALLER WORDS PUT TOGETHER.

A **beehive** is where bees make honey.

Children play with sand in a **sandbox**.

A **hillside** is steep, sloping land.

An astronaut rides in a **spaceship**.

You can cook apples to make **applesauce**.

Homework is an assignment you do at home.

You cross the street at a **crosswalk**.

Trains travel along the tracks of a **railroad**.

A **rowboat** is a small boat that is moved by rowing.

A **turtleneck** is a
long neck.

A. Complete each sentence with a vocabulary word.

1. A ship for space travel is a _____ .

2. The sauce of an apple is _____ .

3. A hive for a bee is a _____ .

4. The side of a hill is a _____ .

5. A large box of sand is a _____ .

B. Use these words to make four vocabulary words.

neck   walk   work   road   cross   turtle   home   rail

1. _____   2. _____

3. _____   4. _____

Compound Words

beehive	**hillside**	**applesauce**	**crosswalk**	**railroad**
sandbox	**spaceship**	**homework**	**turtleneck**	**rowboat**

A. Use what you know. Write the best word to complete each sentence.

1. Leo does his _____ after school each day.

2. The _____ will orbit Earth.

3. Mom made _____ for supper.

4. There is a big _____ at the playground.

5. The boys like to roll down the _____ .

6. You'll get stung if you go near that _____ .

7. Look both ways at the _____ .

8. Sandy is wearing a red sweater with a _____ .

B. Read each question. Choose the best answer.

1. Where can you hear a hum? ❑ beyond ❑ beehive

2. Which is from a fruit? ❑ applesauce ❑ applecart

3. Which one is for school? ❑ housework ❑ homework

4. Which one do you wear? ❑ turtledove ❑ turtleneck

5. Which one needs oars? ❑ motorboat ❑ rowboat

✏ Writing to Learn

Suppose a creature from space visits you. Choose two of the vocabulary words. Explain the words in writing for your visitor.

Compound Words

Write a word for each picture. Then write the compound word.

1.   +   **walk**   =   _____

2. **sand**   +   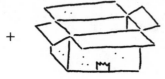   =   _____

3.   +   **hive**   =   _____

4.    +   **side**   =   _____

5. **space**   +      =   _____

6.   +   **sauce**   =   _____

7.    +   **work**   =   _____

8.    +   **neck**   =   _____

Homophones

fur	principle	berry	paws	wail
fir	principal	bury	pause	whale

A **HOMOPHONE** IS A WORD THAT SOUNDS LIKE ANOTHER WORD BUT HAS A DIFFERENT MEANING AND A DIFFERENT SPELLING.

Fur is a covering on many animals.
A **fir** is a kind of evergreen tree.
A **principle** is a rule.
A **principal** is the head of a school.
A dog has **paws** for feet.
If you **pause**, you take a break.
When you **wail**, you cry.
A **whale** is a very large animal that lives in the sea.

berry

bury

A. Complete each riddle with a vocabulary word. Use the picture to help you.

1. I sound like *wail*, but I am a _____ .

2. I sound like *bury*, but I am a _____ .

3. I sound like *fur*, but I am a _____ .

B. Read the words in each row. Then write a vocabulary word that is a synonym.

1. hide, cover, conceal _____   2. cry, weep, moan _____

3. rest, hesitate, linger _____   4. rule, law, ideal _____

NAME _____ DATE _____

Homophones

fur	principle	berry	paws	wail
fir	principal	bury	pause	whale

A. Use what you know. Write the best word to complete each sentence.

1. There will be a short _____ before the show goes on.

2. Todd let out a _____ when he stubbed his toe.

3. Where did that dog _____ its bone?

4. This plant has a red _____ .

5. A blue _____ can grow up to 100 feet long.

6. Being kind is an important _____ in my family.

7. The cat walks very quietly on her _____ .

8. Some animals have scales, and other animals have _____ .

9. A _____ tree has cones and is always green.

10. The _____ visited our classroom.

B. Read each question. Choose the best answer.

1. Which one can you eat? ❑ berry   ❑ bury
2. What does a bear have? ❑ fir   ❑ fur
3. Which one is a sound?   ❑ whale   ❑ wail
4. Which one has paws?   ❑ lion   ❑ snake

✏ Writing to Learn

Choose two vocabulary words. Write a sentence that tells what each word is, and another sentence that tells what each word is *not*.

NAME _____   DATE _____

Homophones

These book titles are all wrong. Rewrite each title so it is correct.

1.

BERRY YOUR TREASURE

_____

_____

_____

2.

Growing
Fur
Trees

_____

_____

_____

3.

ANIMAL PAUSE AND ANIMAL FIR

_____

_____

_____

4.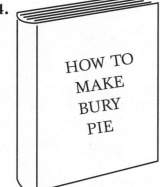

HOW TO
MAKE
BURY
PIE

_____

_____

_____

5.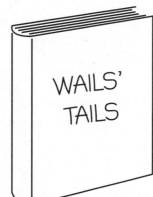

WAILS'
TAILS

_____

_____

_____

6.

Paws
Before
You
Whale

_____

_____

_____

Homophones

ant	**stake**	**peak**	**council**	**threw**
aunt	**steak**	**peek**	**counsel**	**through**

> A **HOMOPHONE** IS A WORD THAT SOUNDS LIKE ANOTHER WORD BUT HAS A DIFFERENT MEANING AND A DIFFERENT SPELLING.

A **stake** is a stick that you drive into the ground.

A **steak** is meat that people eat.

The top of a mountain is a **peak**.

If you **peek** at something, you look at it.

A **council** is a group of people that plans something.

A parent or teacher can **counsel** you about a problem.

Threw is the past tense of *throw*. / You can walk **through** a door.

We both like picnics though!

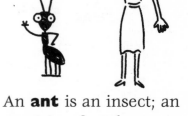

An **ant** is an insect; an **aunt** is a female person.

A. Complete each riddle with a vocabulary word. Use the picture to help you.

1. I sound like *aunt*,

   but I am an _____.

2. I sound like *peek*,

   but I am a _____.

3.  I sound like *stake*,

   but I am a _____.

4.  I sound like *counsel*,

   but I am a _____.

B. Read the words in each row. Then write a vocabulary word that is a synonym.

1. post, stick, pole _____

2. glance, look, see _____

3. tossed, heaved, flung _____

4. advise, discuss, consult _____

Homophones

ant	stake	peak	council	threw
aunt	steak	peek	counsel	through

A. Use what you know. Write the best word to complete each sentence.

1. The bus drove _____ many towns.

2. It took hours for the climbers to reach the _____ .

3. An _____ is a sister of your mother or father.

4. Donna _____ the trash in the basket.

5. The _____ met to elect a new leader.

6. Put a _____ in the ground to mark the boundary.

7. An _____ can carry food that weighs more than it does.

8. Take a _____ at this picture.

9. The president looked to his advisors for _____ .

10. Dad will grill a _____ for supper.

B. Read each question. Choose the best answer.

1. Who is a relative?   ❏ ant   ❏ aunt
2. What's at the top?   ❏ peak   ❏ peek
3. Who threw the ball?   ❏ pitcher   ❏ batter
4. What can you see through?   ❏ wall   ❏ window

 **Writing to Learn**

Choose two vocabulary words. Use them in a comic strip
that you create.

Homophones

These headlines have mistakes. Rewrite them so they are correct.

1. **MAYOR DRIVES FIRST STEAK FOR NEW BUILDING**

   _____

2. *Elephants Parade Threw Town*

   _____

3. First Snowfall Covers High Peek

   _____

4. **ANT THROUGH OUT NEPHEW'S REPORT**

   _____

5. *A Peak at the News*

   _____

6. ***AUNTS FOUND IN STAKE DINNER***

   _____

7. CITY COUNSEL MEETS TODAY

   _____

Homographs

dove	record	live	lead	wind
dove	record	live	lead	wind

> A **HOMOGRAPH** IS A WORD THAT IS SPELLED THE SAME AS ANOTHER WORD BUT HAS A DIFFERENT MEANING AND SOMETIMES A DIFFERENT PRONUNCIATION.

It rhymes with **love**.

A **dove** is a bird.

Dove is a past form of *dive*.

A band can **record** a song.

You can keep a **record** of your grades.

You **live** in a country.

A **live** flower is a living one.

Lead is a kind of metal.

If you **lead** a parade, you are at the beginning of it.

You must **wind** some clocks. / A strong **wind** can knock you down.

It rhymes with **stove**.

A. Read the words in each row. Circle three words that rhyme with the word at left.

1. live	hive	give	dive	five
2. lead	bead	head	bed	sled
3. dove	cove	drove	glove	rove
4. lead	bleed	feed	dead	weed
5. wind	find	grinned	hind	mind

B. Choose the correct word for each sentence. Write *a* or *b* in the blank.

a. rek' ord   **b.** ree kord'

1. A thermometer will _____ the temperature.

2. The judge kept a _____ of the scores.

Homographs

dove	record	live	lead	wind
dove	record	live	lead	wind

A. Use what you know. Write the best word to complete each sentence.

1. The city has a _____ of when you were born.

2. Jane _____ into the lake with a splash.

3. Your address tells where you _____ .

4. Let's _____ the story on tape.

5. The hostess will _____ us to a table.

6. The _____ howled during the storm.

7. Toy soldiers are sometimes made of _____ .

8. The _____ was cooing on its perch.

9. Elise was late because she forgot to _____ her alarm clock.

10. You can see a _____ broadcast of the concert.

B. Read each question. Choose the answer.

1. Which one can you lead? ❑ house   ❑ horse
2. What helps a plant live? ❑ water   ❑ waste
3. Which one has feathers? ❑ dove   ❑ dive
4. Which one is a metal? ❑ lead   ❑ leader

✏️ Writing to Learn

Choose a pair of homographs. Write two questions. The answer for each question should be one of the homographs.

Homographs

Complete the puzzle.

Across
1. show the way
4. the opposite of dead
6. A singer might do this to a song.
7. This metal is used in batteries.
9. This blows during storms.

Down
2. This bird is a symbol of peace.
3. You do this to some clocks.
5. took a plunge
6. a round disk that plays music
8. make a home in a place; reside

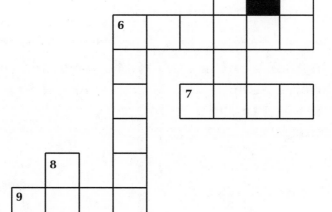

Irregular Plurals

grandchildren	halves	mice	oxen	feet
echoes	geese	mysteries	sketches	sheep

SOME NOUNS HAVE IRREGULAR PLURAL FORMS.

1 mouse
2 mice

1 bird 2 birds

Some noun plurals are **irregular**.

Most noun plurals end in **s**.

The children of someone's children are **grandchildren**.

Sounds that are repeated are **echoes**. / **Halves** are two equal parts of a whole.

Geese are large birds that make a honking sound.

Mysteries are things that are secret or hard to explain.

Oxen are large farm animals in the cattle family.

Quick drawings are called **sketches**. / Our **feet** are at the end of our legs.

Sheep are animals whose fur is used for wool.

A. Match the singular word in the first column to the correct plural word in the second column.

1. echo   **a.** halves

2. grandchild   **b.** mysteries

3. foot   **c.** sheep

4. sketch   **d.** echoes

5. half   **e.** feet

6. mystery   **f.** grandchildren

7. sheep   **g.** sketches

B. Write the plural word for the animal in each picture.

1.  _____

2.  _____

3.  _____

4.  _____

© 240 VOCABULARY WORDS FOR GRADE 3   SCHOLASTIC PROFESSIONAL BOOKS

Irregular Plurals

grandchildren	halves	mice	oxen	feet
echoes	geese	mysteries	sketches	sheep

A. Use what you know. Write the best word to complete each sentence.

1. The artist made _____ before beginning to paint.

2. A team of _____ pulled the hay wagon.

3. The grandparents called their _____ every week.

4. In the fall, wild _____ fly south.

5. The _____ provided the farmer with all the wool she needed.

6. Many people like to read _____ .

7. When sounds bounce off walls, they make _____ .

8. Molly cut the apple into _____ .

9. The cat chased two _____ but caught only one.

10. Sam put his _____ into his new boots.

B. Read each question. Choose the best answer.

1. How do you make sketches?   ❏ write   ❏ draw
2. Which word means "two"?   ❏ halves   ❏ whole
3. Which could be a pair?   ❏ ox   ❏ oxen
4. Which could be a flock?   ❏ goose   ❏ geese

 Writing to Learn

Write a short talk between two people. Use at least two of the vocabulary words.

Irregular Plurals

Play Guess the Rule.
Read each rule. Then write the vocabulary word or words that follow that rule.

1. To form the plural, change the *f* to *v* and add *es*.

_____

2. To form the plural, change the *y* to *i* and add *es*.

_____

3. To form the plural, add *es*.

_____

4. To form the plural, add letters at the end.

_____

5. To form the plural, change the vowels.

_____

6. I don't have a rule. My spelling changes almost completely.

_____

7. I don't have a rule. My spelling doesn't change at all.

_____

Rhyming Words

coast	limb	shriek	fern	glee
host	trim	creek	yearn	plea

▌A WORD THAT HAS THE SAME ENDING SOUND AS
ANOTHER WORD **RHYMES** WITH THAT WORD.

A **coast** is the land along a sea.

The one who gives the party is the **host**.

A branch of a tree is called a **limb**.

When you **trim** something, you cut it.

A **fern** is a kind of plant.

If you long for something, you **yearn** for it.

Glee means "joy."

When you make a **plea** for something, you beg for it.

Eeeek!

A **shriek** from the **creek**.

A. Read the word in the first column. Find and circle two other words
that rhyme with it.

1. **limb**	skim	brim	climb
2. **shriek**	field	tweak	peak
3. **coast**	boast	most	lost
4. **yearn**	year	earn	burn
5. **plea**	sea	free	weigh

B. Read each clue. Write the vocabulary word.

1. Begins like **cr**ow and ends like w**eek**.   _____

2. Begins like **c**ook and ends like t**oast**.   _____

3. Begins like **tr**ee and ends like br**im**.   _____

4. Begins like **pl**ay and ends like **sea**.   _____

Rhyming Words

coast	limb	shriek	fern	glee
host	trim	creek	yearn	plea

A. Use what you know. Write the best word to complete each sentence.

1. Jack will be our _____ for the evening.

2. Mom let out a loud _____ when the vase fell.

3. Does your puppy _____ for you when you're away?

4. Dad hung the swing from a _____ of the tree.

5. The hikers jumped over the _____ and didn't get wet.

6. Javier was filled with _____ at the thought of the party.

7. We saw a green _____ in the woods.

8. The sailboat moved out to sea from the _____ .

9. Brianna made a _____ for a new jacket.

10. Use the scissors to _____ the wrapping paper.

B. Read each question. Choose the best answer.

1. Which one is wet?   ❏ creak   ❏ creek
2. Which one grows?   ❏ fern   ❏ form
3. Which one is an arm?   ❏ limb   ❏ lime
4. Which one is a coast?   ❏ shore   ❏ pool

✐ Writing to Learn

Use two of the vocabulary words in a rhyme.

Rhyming Words

Add vocabulary words that rhyme to the poems.

The Gardener

The gardener got the clippers

For he was going to _____
An old and thorny rose bush

By cutting off a _____ .

The gardener loved his roses,

But never did he _____
For a plant without a flower.

No, he didn't want a _____ .

Fishing

Jody went fishing

Down at the _____ .
She caught such a big fish,

It made Jody _____ !

The Beach Party

Clem had a party

And he was the _____ .
We all went swimming

At Clem's party by the _____ .

Words From Other Languages

pecan	**moose**	**noodle**	**kindergarten**	**bungalow**
squash	**chipmunk**	**pretzel**	**loft**	**dinghy**

■ MANY WORDS IN ENGLISH COME FROM **OTHER LANGUAGES**.

I come from **Germany**.

Native American Words   A **pecan** is a kind of nut.
Squash is a kind of vegetable.
A **moose** is a large animal with antlers.
A **chipmunk** is a small animal something like a squirrel.

Words From German   A **noodle** is made of flour, water, and eggs.
You go to **kindergarten** before starting first grade.

Word From Danish   A **loft** is a room just under the roof of a building.

Words From Hindi   A **bungalow** is a small, one-story house.
A **dinghy** is a small boat.

A. Write *Native American, German, Danish,* or *Hindi* to tell where the word for each picture is from.

1.

_____

2.

_____

3.

_____

4.

_____

5.

_____

6.

_____

B. Read the clue. Write the correct vocabulary word.

1. You can find me at a school.   _____

2. You can find me in a barn.   _____

3. You can find people living in me.   _____

4. You can find me on a lake.   _____

Words From Other Languages

pecan	moose	noodle	kindergarten	bungalow
squash	chipmunk	pretzel	loft	dinghy

A. Use what you know. Write the best word to complete each sentence.

1. We grew _____ in our vegetable garden.

2. A little _____ ran across the yard.

3. Barry bought a salty _____ for a snack.

4. Miss Barnes teaches _____ .

5. A huge _____ came out of the woods.

6. The two boys rowed the _____ across the lake.

7. The farmer stored hay in the _____ of his barn.

8. Grandma makes a tasty _____ pie.

9. We spent our vacation in a _____ near the ocean.

10. Dad is cooking egg _____ for supper.

B. Read each question. Choose the best answer.

1. Which one has a shell?   ❑ pear   ❑ pecan
2. Which one is for children?   ❑ college   ❑ kindergarten
3. Which one is twisted?   ❑ pretzel   ❑ parcel
4. Which one is like a deer?   ❑ mouse   ❑ moose

 Writing to Learn

Write a menu for dinner. Use as many vocabulary words as you can.

Words From Other Languages

Read the clues. Then find and circle each word in the puzzle. Write the word next to its clue.

```
K  C  F  J  I  P  M  X  P  K  D  W  G  X
N  Z  C  L  S  A  E  S  E  T  U  P  O  B
C  A  H  Q  N  E  Y  R  C  D  X  R  N  U
I  K  I  N  D  E  R  G  A  R  T  E  N  N
D  V  P  O  T  X  J  F  N  V  L  T  U  G
I  B  M  O  O  S  E  K  P  O  Q  Z  B  A
N  A  U  D  H  L  C  Z  U  N  K  E  G  L
G  E  N  L  O  F  T  R  J  D  S  L  X  O
H  P  K  E  Z  W  B  V  H  Y  P  H  K  W
Y  C  G  M  E  S  Q  U  A  S  H  B  N  V
```

1. an animal with hooves _____

2. A pumpkin is one. _____

3. a class for five-year-olds _____

4. a Native American word for a small, furry rodent _____

5. a Danish word that rhymes with *soft* _____

6. a nut that grows on trees _____

7. a salty snack food _____

8. a German food made from flour and eggs _____

9. a Hindi word for small house _____

10. a small boat _____

Words From Other Languages

boss	**cookie**	**plaza**	**garage**	**pizza**
drum	**patio**	**ballet**	**menu**	**bravo**

▌MANY WORDS IN ENGLISH COME
FROM **OTHER LANGUAGES.**

I'm a **Dutch** word.

Words From Dutch   The **boss** is the person in charge of a job.
You beat a **drum** to make sounds.

cookie

Words From Spanish   A **patio** is a paved area near a house.
A **plaza** is an open space in a city or town..

Words From French   **Ballet** is a form of dance
You park cars in a **garage**.
A **menu** lists the food served in a restaurant.

Words From Italian   A **pizza** is a kind of pie with cheese and tomatoes on a crust.
Audience members yell "**bravo**" when they like a performance.

A. Write *Dutch, Spanish, French, or Italian* to tell what language the
word for each picture is from.

1.  _____

2. _____

3. _____

4. _____

5.  _____

6. _____

B. Read each clue. Write the correct vocabulary word.

1. You can find me with a work crew.   _____

2. You can find me in the center of a town.   _____

3. You can hear me after a great concert.   _____

4. You can find people relaxing on me just outside
their homes.   _____

Words From Other Languages

boss	cookie	plaza	garage	pizza
drum	patio	ballet	menu	bravo

A. Use what you know. Write the best word to complete each sentence.

1. A _____ is good for dessert.

2. Some towns have a shopping _____ .

3. Dave plays the _____ in the school band.

4. The audience clapped when the _____ was over.

5. We ordered a large _____ with extra cheese.

6. Ari ate breakfast on the _____ .

7. The diners looked at the _____ before ordering.

8. The workers waited for the _____ to explain the job.

9. Mr. Blake drove his car into the _____ .

10. Everyone shouted " _____ " after the speech.

B. Read each question. Choose the best answer.

1. Which one is an instrument? ❏ drum ❏ drop
2. Which one can you read? ❏ menu ❏ meal
3. Which one is a building? ❏ garbage ❏ garage
4. Which one is sweet? ❏ cookie ❏ cracker

🎵 Writing to Learn

Write two sentences about jobs that people do. Use a vocabulary word in each sentence.

Words From Other Languages

Each fortune in these cookies is missing a word. Write a vocabulary word to make each fortune complete.

1. Practice hard, and you will learn to play the _____ well.

2. You will soon win a ticket to see the _____ .

3. It's your lucky day! Mom is serving _____ for dinner tonight.

4. Congratulations! You are about to be promoted to be the _____ at your job.

5. Hurry! You'll find great sales at the shopping _____ today.

6. Beware! You may be asked to help clean out the _____ on Saturday.

7.  Someday you will become a famous chef and plan a great _____ .

8. _____ ! You will give a great performance today.

Clips

bike	exam	bus	zoo	auto
hippo	mitt	lab	sub	math

▌A **CLIP** IS A WORD THAT HAS BEEN
SHORTENED, OR CLIPPED.

I'm a hippopotamus, but many
people call me a **hippo**.

You pedal a **bike** to make its wheels move.

An **exam** is a kind of test.

Baseball players catch balls in a **mitt**.

Do you ride a **bus** to school?

Scientists do research in a **lab**.

A **zoo** is a place where animals are kept.

A **sub** travels on and under the water.

An **auto** is a form of transportation.

In **math**, you study numbers, shapes, measurements, and much more.

A. Draw a line to match each clip to
the word(s) from which it comes.

1. **mitt**   a. mathematics

2. **bus**   b. mitten

3. **math**   c. hippopotamus

4. **sub**   d. automobile

5. **zoo**   e. zoological garden

6. **lab**   f. omnibus

7. **auto**   g. submarine

8. **hippo**   h. laboratory

B. Write the clip for
these words.

1. bicycle

_____

2. examination

_____

Clips

bike	exam	bus	zoo	auto
hippo	mitt	lab	sub	math

A. Use what you know. Write the best word to complete each sentence.

1. The class saw many animals at the _____ .

2. A _____ is a covering for a hand.

3. Scouts who pass the _____ earn a badge.

4. Mr. Nuñez gave the students two pages of _____ homework.

5. Connie rode her _____ to the beach.

6. Dr. Gram did some tests in the _____ .

7. The _____ dove to the bottom of the sea.

8. That _____ is a huge animal.

9. The _____ made several stops before it got to school.

10. Ravi's _____ fit into the small parking space.

B. Read each question. Choose the best answer.

1. What's at a zoo?   ❏ hiccup   ❏ hippo
2. Which one has a driver?   ❏ bass   ❏ bus
3. Which one do you study for?   ❏ exam   ❏ exit
4. Which one is math?   ❏ subtraction   ❏ submarine

 Writing to Learn

Write two math word problems. Use two vocabulary words.

Clips

Read the words in the box. Next to each vocabulary word, write the words from the box that relate to it in some way. You will use some words more than once.

sea	handlebar	ball	scientist	leather	fare
exam	hippo	add	catch	fish	seatbelt
tiger	engine	elephant	divide	headlight	measure
seat	experiment	spoke	monkey	pedal	

1. bus _____

2. bike _____

3. lab _____

4. zoo _____

5. math _____

6. mitt _____

7. auto _____

8. sub _____

Content Words: Young Animals

cub	piglet	calf	cygnet	kid
kit	gosling	foal	fawn	joey

YOUNG ANIMALS OFTEN
HAVE SPECIAL NAMES.

Cub is the word for a young bear, lion, or tiger.

A **kit** is a baby fox.

A baby pig is a **piglet**.

A **gosling** is a baby goose.

The young born to cows, whales, or elephants is called a **calf**.

Foal is the name for a young horse or donkey.

A **cygnet** is a young swan.

The offspring of a goat is a **kid**.

A **joey** is a baby kangaroo.

A young deer is
called a **fawn**.

A. Write the word for each young animal.

1.   _____

2.  _____

3.   _____

4.   _____

5.   _____

6.   _____

B. Write the kind of animal that each one is.

1. **cygnet** _____   2. **fawn** _____

3. **gosling** _____   4. **joey** _____

Content Words: Young Animals

cub	piglet	calf	cygnet	kid
kit	gosling	foal	fawn	joey

A. Use what you know. Write the best word to complete each sentence.

1. The lovely swan watched its _____ swim.

2. The little _____ stayed close to the herd of deer.

3. On a warm day, a cow and a _____ grazed in the field.

4. A _____ ran in the woods followed by a larger fox.

5. The noisy _____ waddled after the mother pig.

6. The lioness licked her _____ .

7. In the spring, this horse will have a _____ .

8. Two goats chased after the _____ .

B. Read each question. Choose the best answer.

1. Which one has a trunk?   ❏ cub   ❏ calf
2. Which one has feathers?   ❏ cygnet   ❏ piglet
3. Which one neighs?   ❏ foal   ❏ fawn
4. Which one is a farm animal?   ❏ kit   ❏ kid
5. Which one lives in its mother's pocket? ❏ joey ❏ gosling
6. Which one honks?   ❏ gosling   ❏ kit

✎ Writing to Learn

Write a sign for a zoo. Use at least two vocabulary words.

NAME _____   DATE _____

Content Words: Young Animals

Read the riddle clues. Write a vocabulary word for each clue.

1. I have stripes and fur. What am I?   _____

2. I have a long neck and webbed feet. What am I?   _____

3. I have hooves and a mane. What am I?   _____

4. I have spots and live in the woods. What am I?   _____

5. I have a bushy tail and live in a den. What am I?   _____

6. I have hooves and go "baaah." What am I?   _____

7. I have a curly tail and live in a pen. What am I?   _____

8. I have flippers and live in the ocean. What am I?   _____

9. I hop and use my tail to balance. What am I?   _____

10. I have feathers and honk. What am I?   _____

Content Words: Ships and Boats

freighter	mast	keel	kayak	deck
helm	wharf	galley	hull	marina

▌ SPECIAL WORDS NAME THINGS RELATING
TO **SHIPS AND BOATS.**

A **mast** is a tall pole that supports a boat's sails.

A ship that carries cargo is a **freighter**.

The **helm** of a ship is a wheel used for steering.

A **wharf** is where a ship docks to load or unload.

The **keel** is the long beam on the bottom center of a ship.

The kitchen on a boat is called the **galley**. / A **kayak** is a kind of canoe.

The body of a boat is the **hull**. / The **deck** is the floor of a boat or ship.

A **marina** is a place where people keep their boats.

A. Read each sentence. Write the vocabulary word that it describes.

1. You paddle me. _____

2. You ship things on me. _____

3. You cook in me. _____

4. You anchor at me. _____

5. You steer me. _____

6. You put sails on me. _____

7. You walk on me. _____

8. You find me on the very bottom of a ship. _____

B. Read each vocabulary word. Circle two other words that mean the same thing.

1. **wharf**   pier   dock   rudder

2. **hull**   casing   gangplank   shell

Content Words: Ships and Boats

freighter	**mast**	**keel**	**kayak**	**deck**
helm	**wharf**	**galley**	**hull**	**marina**

A. Use what you know. Write the best word to complete each sentence.

1. About 100 sailboats are kept at this _____ .

2. The camper paddled along in her _____ .

3. There are cold drinks and sandwiches in the _____ .

4. The captain stood at the _____ to steer.

5. Part of a boat's _____ is in the water.

6. The longest piece of wood on a boat is the _____ .

7. Sailors hung rigging from the tall _____ .

8. Last summer, we fished off this _____ .

9. A large _____ carried cars across the ocean.

10. The waves splashed over the _____ and made it slippery.

B. Read each question. Choose the best answer.

1. Which one has a sink?   ❏ galley   ❏ gallery
2. What's the helm for?   ❏ stirring   ❏ steering
3. Which one is smaller?   ❏ kayak   ❏ freighter
4. Which one can you climb?   ❏ mess   ❏ mast
5. Which one can you walk on?   ❏ keel   ❏ deck

 **Writing to Learn**

Draw a picture of a boat or ship. Label the parts using at least two vocabulary words.

Content Words: Ships and Boats

Use the vocabulary words to fill in the map.

Kinds

1. _____

2. _____

**Boats
and Ships**

Parts

3. _____

4. _____

5. _____

6. _____

7. _____

8. _____

Places

9. _____

10. _____

Root Words *nav* and *form*

navy	**navigate**	**formula**	**reform**	**uniform**
naval	**navigable**	**conform**	**transform**	**format**

▌SOME WORDS SHARE
THE **SAME ROOT**.

All of a nation's warships
are in its **navy**.

Root:

Nav means "ship."   Things relating to a navy are **naval**.

If you **navigate** a ship, you direct its course.

If a river is **navigable**, boats can sail on it.

Form means "shape."   A **formula** explains how to prepare a mixture.

If you **conform**, you act in a way that agrees with the rules.

When you **reform** something, you make it better.

Transform means "to change in some way."

When something is **uniform**, it is always the same.

A **format** is the size and shape something takes.

A. Read the vocabulary word. Find and circle two other words that
mean almost the same thing.

1. **conform**   agree   accord   annoy

2. **navigate**   sail   relate   cruise

3. **transform**   alter   change   send

4. **uniform**   steady   irregular   unchanging

5. **reform**   refer   improve   correct

B. Underline the root in each word.

1. **naval**   2. **formula**   3. **navy**   4. **format**

NAME _____ DATE _____

Root Words *nav* and *form*

navy	navigate	formula	reform	uniform
naval	navigable	conform	transform	format

A. Use what you know. Write the best word to complete each sentence.

1. The mayor wants to _____ the government to make it better.

2. A _____ is an outfit that is the same for everyone.

3. A sailor serves in the _____ .

4. The scientists developed a _____ for a new medicine.

5. The captain will _____ the ship into port.

6. The students decided on a new _____ for the talent show.

7. A new coat of paint would _____ this drab room.

8. There is a _____ base near this town.

9. Students should _____ to the rules at school.

10. The large ship had to turn around because the river was not

_____ .

B. Read each question. Choose the best answer.

1. Which one can you wear? ❑ unicycle   ❑ uniform
2. How do you conform? ❑ accept   ❑ reject
3. Which one is a recipe? ❑ formula   ❑ fortune
4. Which one can you join? ❑ naval   ❑ navy

 **Writing to Learn**

Explain why it is helpful to know the root of a word. Use two
vocabulary words as examples.

Root Words *nav* and *form*

Use the clues to complete the puzzle.

Across
1. describing navy things
2. a country's armed forces at sea
6. remake in some way
7. change to improve
8. a river large and deep enough for ships to travel on
9. the shape and size of something

Down
1. related to the word *navigation*
3. what a conformist does
4. a plan for making or doing something
5. a police officer wears one

Noisy Words

buzz	clank	sizzle	purr	rattle
boom	murmur	crash	hum	bleat

▌ SOME WORDS SUGGEST
▌ **SOUNDS.**

I purr.

Many insects **buzz**.

A drum sound can be a deep **boom**.

A **clank** is a sharp sound made by metal hitting metal.

A **murmur** is a soft and gentle sound. / A **sizzle** is a hissing sound.

A **crash** is a sudden, loud noise. / If you **hum**, you make a droning sound.

A **rattle** is a series of short, sharp sounds. / Goats and sheep **bleat**.

A. Read each sentence. Write the best word to describe the sound.

1. drop a baking pan _____

2. shake a baby's toy _____

3. fry bacon _____

4. light dynamite _____

5. pet a goat _____

6. feed a kitten _____

7. speak softly _____

8. sing without saying words _____

B. Circle the correct answer to each question.

1. Which one can clank?   bike chain   bike bell   bike tire

2. Which one can buzz?   doorknob   doormat   doorbell

Noisy Words

buzz	**clank**	**sizzle**	**purr**	**rattle**
boom	**murmur**	**crash**	**hum**	**bleat**

A. Use what you know. Write the best word to complete each sentence.

1. When the ball broke the window, there was a loud _____ .

2. The _____ of the snake scared us.

3. Kirk woke to the _____ of his alarm clock.

4. If you don't know the words to the song, you can _____ .

5. When drops of water hit something hot, you hear a _____ .

6. A soft _____ came from Zoe's cat when she stroked it.

7. Toby heard a _____ as the tow truck driver let out his chains.

8. The _____ of the explosion was heard for miles around.

B. Read each question. Choose the best answer.

1. Which one is loud? ❑ purr ❑ crash

2. Which one is sharp? ❑ hum ❑ rattle

3. Which one is deep? ❑ boom ❑ buzz

4. Which one can sizzle? ❑ rainbow ❑ radiator

5. Which one can bleat? ❑ owl ❑ sheep

6. Which one is gentle? ❑ murmur ❑ roar

 **Writing to Learn**

Draw a comic with lots of noise and action. Use at least two vocabulary words.

Noisy Words

Look at the pictures. Then write a sound word in each speech balloon.

1.

2.

3.

4.

5.

6.

7.

8.

9.

10.

Word Stories

teddy bear	vandal	atlas	capital	ritzy
salt	watt	cereal	muscle	palace

▌MANY WORDS HAVE INTERESTING
STORIES ABOUT THEIR ORIGINS.

The **teddy bear** is named for a U.S. President, Theodore (Teddy) Roosevelt.

Salt is a seasoning used to flavor and preserve food.

A **vandal** is someone who destroys something on purpose.

A **watt** is a measure of electric power. / An **atlas** is a book of maps.

Cereal is a breakfast food made from grains such as wheat and corn.

The **capital** of a state or country is where government heads meet.

A **muscle** is a tissue in your body made of strong fiber.

Ritzy means "very fancy." / A **palace** is a grand home for a king or queen.

A. Write a vocabulary word for each word story.

1. The Latin word *musculus* means "little mouse." _____

2. The Latin word *caput* means "head." _____

3. In ancient Rome, there were fine homes on Palatine Hill. _____

4. *Sal* (a Latin word) was a highly valued substance long ago. _____

5. In ancient Europe, the Vandals were known for attacking and stealing from neighboring groups of people. _____

B. Draw a line from each vocabulary word to the person for which it is named.

1. **watt**   a. Ceres was the Roman goddess who protected crops.

2. **atlas**   b. Theodore Roosevelt once saved a bear cub on a hunting trip.

3. **cereal**   c. Cesar Ritz owned a very fancy hotel in Switzerland.

4. **teddy bear** d. In Greek myths, Atlas was a giant who had to hold the world on his shoulders.

5. **ritzy**   e. James Watt was an inventor who worked on ways to develop power for machines.

Word Stories

teddy bear	vandal	atlas	capital	ritzy
salt	watt	cereal	muscle	palace

A. Use what you know. Write the best word to complete each sentence.

1. The _____ is a soft and popular toy.

2. You need a 60- _____ bulb for that lamp.

3. The princess lived in a beautiful _____ with many rooms.

4. Salami and sausage are two meats with _____ in them.

5. What kind of _____ do you eat for breakfast?

6. Washington, D.C., is the _____ of the United States.

7. You'll find maps of the continents in an _____ .

8. To move your body, you need _____ .

9. The police found the _____ responsible for destroying the road sign.

10. Alex has a _____ box covered with gold and jewels.

B. Read each question. Choose the best answer.

1. Which one can you hug? ❏ grizzly bear ❏ teddy bear
2. Which one is a capital? ❏ Miami, FL ❏ Tallahassee, FL
3. Which one is a home? ❏ palace ❏ palomino
4. Which goes with pepper? ❏ salt ❏ sail
5. Which one might be ritzy? ❏ hotel ❏ junkyard

✍ Writing to Learn

Find out more about the story behind one of the vocabulary words. Write a paragraph to explain its background.

Word Stories

Complete a chain for each word. In each circle, write a word that is related to the word just before it. An example is done for you.

(**cereal**)(breakfast)(morning)(hurry)(school)

1. (**watt**)( )( )( )( )

2. (**muscle**)( )( )( )( )

3. (**salt**)( )( )( )( )

4. (**palace**)( )( )( )( )

5. (**teddy bear**)( )( )( )( )

6. (**capital**)( )( )( )( )

7. (**atlas**)( )( )( )( )

8. (**vandal**)( )( )( )( )

9. (**ritzy**)( )( )( )( )

Prefixes *mis-, in-, sub-, un-, re-*

misbehave	**indirect**	**subtitle**	**unfold**	**recount**
mistrust	**informal**	**subtotal**	**unequal**	**review**

▎A **PREFIX** IS A WORD PART THAT IS ADDED TO THE BEGINNING OF A WORD. A PREFIX CHANGES THE MEANING OF A WORD.

mis- means "badly"
in- and *un-* mean "not"
sub- means "under"
re- means "again"

The hamburgers are not the same size, so they are **unequal**.

If you **misbehave**, you act badly.

If you **mistrust** someone, you doubt that person.

If something is **indirect**, it is roundabout. / You wear **informal** clothes for play.

A **subtitle** is below the main title. / A **subtotal** is not the whole total.

When you **unfold** something, you open it up.

Recount means "to count again."

When you **review** something, you look at it once more.

A. Add a prefix to each word to form a vocabulary word. Use the meaning in ( ) to help you.

1. (again) _____ view   **2.** (under) _____ total

3. (not) _____ formal   **4.** (not) _____ equal

5. (badly) _____ behave   **6.** (under) _____ title

B. Write a heading that tells how the words in each group are alike.

1. _____   **2.** _____   **3.** _____   **4.** _____

indirect	misname	unfair	recount
incorrect	mistrust	unzip	renew
insecure	miscast	unfold	redo

Prefixes mis-, in-, sub-, un-, re-

misbehave	indirect	subtitle	unfold	recount
mistrust	informal	subtotal	unequal	review

A. Use what you know. Write the best word to complete each sentence.

1. Our dog will _____ if we don't train him.

2. The _____ light made it hard to read.

3. This magazine story has a long _____ .

4. The jars had _____ amounts of water.

5. The clerk made a mistake and had to _____ my change.

6. Always _____ the material before taking a test.

7. The Blakes had an _____ party in their yard.

8. Gina had to _____ the blanket before using it.

9. The _____ on this order is six dollars.

10. If you are not honest, people will _____ you.

B. Read each question. Choose the best answer.

1. Which one is informal? ❏ tuxedo ❏ sweatsuit
2. Which one isn't fair? ❏ unequal ❏ equal
3. Whom do you mistrust? ❏ liar ❏ friend
4. Which one do you unfold? ❏ leader ❏ letter

 Writing to Learn

Explain how one of the prefixes changes the meaning of words.
Use at least two vocabulary words in your explanation.

Prefixes mis-, in-, sub-, un-, re-

Find the hidden picture. Cut out the squares on the right side of the page. Match the word on each square to the correct meaning on the left side of the page. Paste the squares to form a picture.

act up	casual
not straight	suspect someone
not equal	a kind of heading
another look	not the final amount
a second count	spread out

recount

unequal

informal

subtitle

unfold

indirect

subtotal

review

misbehave

mistrust

Prefixes *mis-, in-, sub-, un-, re-*

| mislead | inactive | subnormal | uncover | renew |
| misplace | invisible | submarine | uneasy | recall |

A **PREFIX** IS A WORD PART THAT IS ADDED TO THE BEGINNING OF A WORD. A PREFIX CHANGES THE MEANING OF A WORD.

mis- means "badly"   *in-* and *un-* mean "not"
sub- means "under"   *re-* means "again"

If you **mislead** people, you give them the wrong idea.

When you **misplace** something, you can't find it.

If you are **inactive**, you no longer do something.

If you are **invisible**, no one can see you.

Something that is **subnormal** is below average.

A **submarine** moves under the water.

When you **uncover** something, you reveal it.

If you begin again, you **renew** something. / **Recall** means "remember."

If you are **uneasy**, you are not sure.

A. Read the word in the first column. Find and circle two other words that mean almost the same thing.

1. **recall**	forget	remember	recollect
2. **inactive**	retired	idle	busy
3. **invisible**	inside	hidden	unseen
4. **uncover**	show	erase	reveal
5. **misplace**	lose	mislay	find

B. Write a heading that tells how the words in each group are alike.

1. _____   2. _____   3. _____   4. _____

subnormal	untold	renew	misuse
sublet	uneasy	recover	mislead
submarine	unlike	rejoin	misread

Prefixes *mis-, in-, sub-, un-, re-*

| mislead | inactive | subnormal | uncover | renew |
| misplace | invisible | submarine | uneasy | recall |

A. Use what you know. Write the best word to complete each sentence.

1. It's time to _____ my library card.

2. Jo was _____ about walking home alone.

3. The _____ began its trip under the sea.

4. Do you _____ what time this class begins?

5. Since his accident, Dan is an _____ member of the club.

6. In the fog, the other cars were almost _____ .

7. She was so cold that she had a _____ temperature.

8. Did Dad _____ his glasses again?

9. The detective hopes to _____ some clues.

10. Choose your words carefully so you don't _____ people.

B. Read each question. Choose the best answer.

1. Which one can you renew? ❒ passport ❒ passenger
2. Which one is invisible? ❒ ghost ❒ guest
3. Which one is a ship? ❒ subnormal ❒ submarine
4. Which one can mislead? ❒ trick ❒ truck

🖋 Writing to Learn

Write a book cover blurb for a mystery story. Use at least two vocabulary words.

Prefixes *mis-*, *in-*, *sub-*, *un-*, *re-*

Here's a challenge for you. Write at least four words that begin with
each prefix. Use one of the words from each group in a sentence.

1. *in-*   _____

_____   _____

_____   _____

_____

2. *un-*   _____

_____   _____

_____   _____

_____

3. *sub-*   _____

_____   _____

_____   _____

_____

4. *mis-*   _____

_____   _____

_____   _____

_____

5. *re-*   _____

_____   _____

_____   _____

_____

Suffixes -ness, -ful, -ly, -ment, -er

dark**ness**	grace**ful**	**distantly**	govern**ment**	rancher
forgive**ness**	plenti**ful**	**rapidly**	amaze**ment**	catcher

A **SUFFIX** IS A WORD PART THAT IS ADDED TO THE END OF A WORD. A SUFFIX CHANGES THE MEANING OF THE WORD.

-*ness* and -*ment* mean "a state of being"
-*ful* means "full of"
-*ly* means "in that way"
-*er* means "a person who acts as"

When there is no light, there is **darkness**.

If you forgive someone, you show **forgiveness**.

A dancer is **graceful**.

You see something **distantly** when it is far away. / **Rapidly** means "quickly."

A **government** runs a city, state, or nation.

You show **amazement** when something surprises you.

A **rancher** works on a ranch. / A **catcher** is a member of a baseball team.

When something is **plentiful**, there is a lot of it.

A. Add a suffix to each word to form a vocabulary word. Use the meaning in ( ) to help you.

1. (state of being) dark _____
2. (one who does something) catch _____
3. (state of being) forgive _____
4. (one who does something) ranch _____
5. (in that way) distant _____
6. (state of being) govern _____

B. Read the words in each row. Write a vocabulary word that means almost the same thing.

1. fast, speedily, quickly _____

2. surprise, astonishment, shock _____

3. much, lots, boundless _____

4. beautiful, elegant, charming _____

Suffixes -ness, -ful, -ly, -ment, -er

dark**ness**	grace**ful**	distant**ly**	govern**ment**	ranch**er**
forgive**ness**	plenti**ful**	rapid**ly**	amaze**ment**	catch**er**

A. Use what you know. Write the best word to complete each sentence.

1. Food was _____ at the picnic.

2. Brad stared in _____ at Tom's crazy costume.

3. The _____ waited for the next pitch.

4. The streetlights went on as _____ fell.

5. The President is head of the United States _____ .

6. From the shore, Mack could see the ships _____ .

7. Kim's brother showed _____ when she forgot his birthday.

8. The _____ keeps a herd of horses.

9. A _____ model walked down the runway.

10. People walked _____ to catch the train.

B. Read each question. Choose the best answer.

1. When do you see stars?   ❏ daytime   ❏ darkness

2. Which one is at home?   ❏ catcher   ❏ pitcher

3. What's not clumsy?   ❏ graceful   ❏ grateful

4. Which one runs rapidly?   ❏ hair   ❏ hare

Writing to Learn

Write a story about a feast. Use at least three vocabulary words in it.

Suffixes -ness, -ful, -ly, -ment, -er

Read the clues. Then find and circle each word in the puzzle. Write the word next to its clue.

```
G  C  X  F  W  B  K  Y  C  J  L  D
R  H  D  M  R  T  L  N  A  Q  P  A
A  M  A  Z  E  M  E  N  T  Z  T  R
C  K  R  T  G  P  J  L  C  P  D  K
E  F  D  U  Z  T  V  R  H  B  I  N
F  O  R  G  I  V  E  N  E  S  S  E
U  J  R  A  N  C  H  E  R  D  T  S
L  H  Y  J  M  S  Q  G  I  N  A  S
Q  D  G  O  V  E  R  N  M  E  N  T
A  Q  Y  B  H  C  P  S  C  O  T  Z
E  X  P  L  E  N  T  I  F  U  L  B
O  W  R  M  R  A  P  I  D  L  Y  H
```

1. a great deal of something _____

2. opposite of light _____

3. a person with a mitt _____

4. It makes the laws. _____

5. an owner of cattle _____

6. heard far away _____

7. full of grace _____

8. wonderment _____

9. in haste _____

10. when something is forgiven _____

© 240 VOCABULARY WORDS FOR GRADE 3 SCHOLASTIC PROFESSIONAL BOOKS

Suffixes -ness, -ful, -ly, -ment, -er

awareness	**tact**ful	**recent**ly	**arrange**ment	**perform**er
laziness	**fright**ful	**quiet**ly	**content**ment	**train**er

▌ A **SUFFIX** IS A WORD PART THAT IS ADDED TO THE END OF
A WORD. A SUFFIX CHANGES THE MEANING OF A WORD.

-ness and *-ment* mean "a state of being"
-ful means "full of"
-ly means "in that way"
-er means "a person who acts as"

A clown is a
performer in
a circus.

Awareness means "being mindful of something."

If you are unwilling to work, you show **laziness**.

Tactful means "thoughtful."   /   **Frightful** means "alarming."

Recently means "it just happened."   /   **Quietly** means "without noise."

An **arrangement** is a plan.   /   When you are pleased, you show **contentment**.

A **trainer** is a teacher.

A. Read the word in the first column. Find and circle two other words
that mean almost the same thing.

1. **frightful**	frightening	shocking	fanciful
2. **contentment**	courage	satisfaction	pleasure
3. **awareness**	knowledge	awful	mindfulness
4. **trainer**	student	teacher	instructor
5. **recently**	newly	lately	ancient
6. **arrangement**	approval	plan	agreement

B. Write a heading that tells how the words in each group are alike.

1. _____	2. _____	3. _____	4. _____
grateful	happiness	performer	loudly
tactful	laziness	runner	nicely
lawful	sadness	writer	quietly

Suffixes -ness, -ful, -ly, -ment, -er

aware**ness**	**frightful**	**recently**	arrange**ment**	perform**er**
lazi**ness**	**tactful**	**quietly**	content**ment**	train**er**

A. Use what you know. Write the best word to complete each sentence.

1. With great _____ , Mom put up her feet and read the paper.

2. _____ , the weather has been very hot.

3. Mr. Sands was _____ when a student made a mistake.

4. After rolling in the mud, the dog looked just _____ .

5. The _____ bowed when people clapped.

6. Eve made an _____ to meet her friend on the corner.

7. The nurse walked _____ down the hall.

8. The team worked with a _____ to prepare for the game.

9. It shows _____ when you don't do your chores.

10. The baby already has an _____ of his family.

B. Read each question. Choose the best answer.

1. Which one is an actress?   ❏ performer   ❏ perfumer
2. What do you do quietly?   ❏ stamp   ❏ tiptoe
3. Which one is tactful?   ❏ rudeness   ❏ politeness
4. When was yesterday?   ❏ recently   ❏ tomorrow

✒ Writing to Learn

Make a poster for a circus. Use at least three vocabulary words.

Suffixes -ness, -ful, -ly, -ment, -er

Here's a challenge for you. Write at least four words that end with each suffix. Use one of the words from each group in a sentence.

1. *-ful* _____

_____   _____

_____   _____

_____

2. *-er* _____

_____   _____

_____   _____

_____

3. *-ly* _____

_____   _____

_____   _____

_____

4. *-ness* _____

_____   _____

_____   _____

_____

5. *-ment* _____

_____   _____

_____   _____

_____

Word List

absent, p. 6
adult, p. 15
amazement, p. 72
annual, p. 6
ant, p. 30
applesauce, p. 24
arrangement,
    p. 75
assist, p. 12
atlas, p. 63
attic, p. 18
aunt, p. 30
auto, p. 48
awareness, p. 75

ballet, p. 45
banner, p. 9
beehive, p. 24
berry, p. 27
bike, p. 48
birdbath, p. 21
bleat, p. 60
boom, p. 60
borrow, p. 18
boss, p. 45
bothersome, p. 12
bravo, p. 45
break, p. 15
bright, p. 18
bungalow, p. 42
bury, p. 27
bus, p. 48
buzz, p. 60

calf, p. 51
capital, p. 63
catcher, p. 72
catfish, p. 21
cellar, p. 18
cereal, p. 63
chipmunk, p. 42
clank, p. 60
coast, p. 39
conform, p. 57
contentment,
    p. 75
cookie, p. 45
council, p. 30
counsel, p. 30
crash, p. 60
creek, p. 39
crosswalk, p. 24

cub, p. 51
cygnet, p. 51

darkness, p. 72
deck, p. 54
deep, p. 15
dim, p. 18
dinghy, p. 42
distantly, p. 72
dove, p. 33
dove, p. 33
drowsy, p. 6
drum, p. 45

echoes, p. 36
exam, p. 48
eyelid, p. 21

fawn, p. 51
feeble, p. 6
feet, p. 36
fern, p. 39
fir, p. 27
flexible, p. 15
foal, p. 51
foe, p. 6
forgiveness, p. 72
format, p. 57
formula, p. 57
frayed, p. 12
freighter, p. 54
frightful, p. 75
fur, p. 27
furious, p. 12

galley, p. 54
garage, p. 45
geese, p. 36
glee, p. 39
gosling, p. 51
government, p. 72
graceful, p. 72
gracious, p. 18
grandchildren,
    p. 36

hairbrush, p. 21
halves, p. 36
helm, p. 54
hillside, p. 24
hippo, p. 48
homework, p. 24
host, p. 39
hull, p. 54

hum, p. 60

ill, p. 9
inactive, p. 69
indirect, p. 66
infant, p. 15
informal, p. 66
invisible, p. 69

joey, p. 51

kayak, p. 54
keel, p. 54
keyboard, p. 21
kid, p. 51
kindergarten,
    p. 42
kit, p. 51

lab, p. 48
laziness, p. 75
lead, p. 33
lead, p. 33
lend, p. 18
limb, p. 39
live, p. 33
live, p. 33
loft, p. 42
loyal, p. 9
lunchtime, p. 21
lurk, p. 12

mammoth, p. 12
marina, p. 54
mast, p. 54
math, p. 48
meadow, p. 9
menu, p. 45
mice, p. 36
misbehave, p. 66
mislead, p. 69
misplace, p. 69
mistrust, p. 66
mitt, p. 48
moose, p. 42
murmur, p. 60
muscle, p. 63
mysteries, p. 36

naval, p. 57
navigable, p. 57
navigate, p. 57
navy, p. 57
noodle, p. 42

orbit, p. 12
overcast, p. 12
oxen, p. 36

pain, p. 15
palace, p. 63
patio, p. 45
pause, p. 27
paws, p. 27
peak, p. 30
pecan, p. 42
peek, p. 30
performer, p. 75
piglet, p. 51
pizza, p. 45
plaza, p. 45
plea, p. 39
pleasure, p. 15
plentiful, p. 72
prank, p. 6
pretzel, p. 42
principal, p. 27
principle, p. 27
purchase, p. 6
purr, p. 60

quietly, p. 75

railroad, p. 24
rainbow, p. 21
rancher, p. 72
rapidly, p. 72
rattle, p. 60
recall, p. 69
recently, p. 75
record, p. 33
record, p. 33
recount, p. 66
reform, p. 57
renew, p. 69
repair, p. 15
reply, p. 6
review, p. 66
rigid, p. 15
ritzy, p. 63
rowboat, p. 24
rude, p. 18

salt, p. 63
sandbox, p. 24
scorekeeper, p. 21
shallow, p. 15
sheep, p. 36
shiver, p. 9

shriek, p. 39
sizzle, p. 60
sketches, p. 36
sloppy, p. 18
slosh, p. 12
slumber, p. 9
spaceship, p. 24
springboard, p. 21
squash, p. 42
stake, p. 30
stalk, p. 9
steak, p. 30
sturdy, p. 6
sub, p. 48
submarine, p. 69
subnormal, p. 69
subtitle, p. 66
subtotal, p. 66

tactful, p. 75
task, p. 12
teddy bear, p. 63
threw, p. 30
through, p. 30
tidy, p. 18
trainer, p. 75
transform, p. 57
trim, p. 39
turtleneck, p. 24

uncover, p. 69
uneasy, p. 69
unequal, p. 66
unfold, p. 66
uniform, p. 57

vacant, p. 9
vandal, p. 63
vast, p. 6
voyage, p. 9

wail, p. 27
waterfall, p. 21
watt, p. 63
whale, p. 27
wharf, p. 54
wild, p. 9
wind, p. 33
wind, p. 33

yearn, p. 39

zoo, p. 48

Answers

Lesson 1, page 6: A. 1. joke, trick 2. enemy, opponent 3. answer, respond 4. weak, frail 5. sleepy, tired 6. strong, tough 7. huge, enormous **B.** 1. here 2. dunk **page 7: A.** 1. annual 2. purchase 3. reply 4. sturdy 5. absent 6. foe 7. feeble 8. prank 9. vast 10. drowsy **B.** 1. buyer 2. pal 3. absent 4. birthday **page 8:** 1. reply 2. feeble 3. drowsy 4. foe 5. annual 6. purchase 7. absent 8. prank

Lesson 2, page 9: A. 1. f. 2. c. 3. e. 4. a. 5. g. 6. b. 7. d. **B.** 1. banner 2. stalk 3. wild **page 10: A.** 1. shiver 2. wild 3. voyage 4. banner 5. slumber 6. loyal 7. stalk 8. meadow 9. ill 10. vacant **B.** 1. meadow 2. celery 3. traveler 4. fear **page 11:** 1-2, 4-5, 7 are synonyms. Possible answers: 3. faithful 6. flag 8. journey 9. empty 10. sick

Lesson 3, page 12: A. 1-8: Answers will vary. **B.** 1. upset, mad 2. annoying, difficult **page 13: A.** 1. task 2. orbit 3. frayed 4. slosh 5. bothersome 6. overcast 7. furious 8. mammoth 9. lurk **B.** 1. mammoth 2. task 3. slosh 4. assist

page 14: Across: 2. furious 4. frayed 5. task 8. overcast 9. bothersome 10. assist; Down: 1. lurk 3. orbit 6. slosh 7. mammoth

Lesson 4, page 15: A. 1. joy 2. destroy 3. grownup 4. deep 5. restore 6. flexible **B.** 1. repair 2. adult 3. pleasure **page 16: A.** 1. infant 2. shallow 3. pleasure 4. adult 5. repair 6. deep 7. rigid 8. break 9. flexible 10. pain **B.** 1. adult 2. pleasure 3. shallow 4. repair **page 17:** deep, repair, pleasure, adult

Lesson 5, page 18: A. 1. d. 2. e. 3. b. 4. a. 5. c. **B.** 1. lend, borrow 2. loft, cellar 3. sloppy, orderly **page 19: A.** 1. cellar 2. tidy 3. bright 4. gracious 5. sloppy 6. borrow 7. dim 8. attic 9. rude 10. lend **B.** 1. cellar 2. slob 3. dim 4. borrow **page 20:** 1. messy, sloppy, disorderly 2. shiny, brilliant, bright 3. receive, borrow, obtain 4. faint, dim, dark 5. neat, orderly, tidy

Lesson 6, page 21: A. 1. hairbrush 2. catfish 3. eyelid 4. lunchtime 5. birdbath **B.** 1. water, fall 2. rain, bow 3. key, board 4. spring, board 5. score, keeper **page 22: A.** 1. keyboard 2. birdbath 3. eyelid 4. rainbow 5. lunchtime 6. hairbrush 7. scorekeeper 8. catfish 9. waterfall 10. springboard **B.** 1. catfish 2. lunchtime 3. keyboard 4. eyelid **page 23:** 1. rainbow 2. keyboard 3. catfish 4. hairbrush 5. birdbath 6. eyelid 7. lunchtime 8. waterfall

Lesson 7, page 24: A. 1. spaceship 2. applesauce 3. beehive 4. hillside 5. sandbox **B.** 1-4 crosswalk, homework, turtleneck, railroad **page 25: A.** 1. homework 2. spaceship 3. applesauce 4. sandbox 5. hillside 6. beehive 7. crosswalk 8. turtleneck **B.** 1. beehive 2. applesauce 3. homework 4. turtleneck 5. rowboat **page 26:** 1. crosswalk 2. sandbox 3. beehive 4. hillside 5. spaceship 6. applesauce 7. homework 8. turtleneck

Lesson 8, page 27: A. 1. whale 2. berry 3. fir **B.** 1.bury 2. wail 3. pause 4. principle **page 28: A.** 1. pause 2. wail 3. bury 4. berry 5. whale 6. principle 7. paws 8. fur 9. fir 10. principal **B.** 1. berry 2. fur 3. wail 4. lion **page 29:** 1. Bury Your Treasure 2. Growing Fir Trees 3. Animal Paws and Animal Fur 4. How to Make Berry Pie 5. Whales' Tails 6. Pause Before You Wail

Lesson 9, page 30: A. 1. ant 2. peak 3. steak 4. council **B.** 1. stake 2. peek 3. threw 4. counsel **page 31: A.** 1. through 2. peak 3. aunt 4. threw 5. council 6. stake 7. ant 8. peek 9. counsel 10. steak **B.** 1. aunt 2. peak 3. pitcher 4. window **page 32:** 1. Mayor Drives First Stake for New Building 2. Elephants Parade Through Town 3. First Snowfall Covers High Peak 4. Aunt Threw Out Nephew's Report 5. A Peek at the News 6. Ants Found in Steak Dinner 7. City Council Meets Today

Lesson 10, page 33: A. 1. hive, dive, five 2. head, bed, sled 3. cove, drove, rove 4. bleed, feed, weed 5. find, hind, mind **B.** 1. b. 2. a. **page 34: A.** 1. record 2. dove 3. live 4. record 5. lead 6. wind 7. lead 8. dove 9. wind 10. live **B.** 1. horse 2. water 3. dove 4. lead

page 35: Across: 1. lead 4. live 6. record 7. lead 9. wind Down: 2. dove 3. wind 5. dove 6. record 8. live

Lesson 11, page 36: A. 1. d. 2. f. 3. e. 4. g. 5. a. 6. b. 7. c. **B.** 1. oxen 2. geese 3. mice 4. sheep **page 37: A.** 1. sketches 2. oxen 3. grandchildren 4. geese 5. sheep 6. mysteries 7. echoes 8. halves 9. mice 10. feet **B.** 1. draw 2. halves 3. oxen 4. geese **page 38:** 1. halves 2. mysteries 3. sketches, echoes 4. oxen, grandchildren 5. geese, feet 6. mice 7. sheep

Lesson 12, page 39: A. 1. skim, brim 2. tweak, peak 3. boast, most 4. earn, burn 5. sea, free **B.** 1. creek 2. coast 3. trim 4. plea **page 40: A.** 1. host 2. shriek 3. yearn 4. limb 5. creek 6. glee 7. fern 8. coast 9. plea 10. trim **B.** 1. creek 2. fern 3. limb 4. shore **page 41:** The Gardener: trim, limb; yearn, fern. Fishing: creek, shriek. The Beach Party: host, coast

Lesson 13, page 42: A. 1. German 2. Native American 3. German 4. Native American 5. Native American 6. Native American **B.** 1. kindergarten 2. loft 3. bungalow 4. dinghy **page 43: A.** 1. squash 2. chipmunk 3. pretzel 4. kindergarten 5. moose 6. dinghy 7. loft 8. pecan 9. bungalow 10. noodles **B.** 1. pecan 2. kindergarten 3. pretzel 4. moose **page 44:** 1. moose 2. squash 3. kindergarten 4. chipmunk 5. loft 6. pecan 7. pretzel 8. noodle 9. bungalow 10. dinghy

Lesson 14, page 45: A. 1. French 2. French 3. Italian 4. French 5. Dutch 6. Dutch **B.** 1. boss 2. plaza 3. bravo 4. patio **page 46: A.** 1. cookie 2. plaza 3. drum 4. ballet 5. pizza 6. patio 7. menu 8. boss 9. garage 10. bravo **B.** 1. drum 2. menu 3. garage 4. cookie **page 47:** 1. drum 2. ballet 3. pizza 4. boss 5. plaza 6. garage 7. menu 8. Bravo

Lesson 15, page 48: A. 1. b. 2. f. 3. a. 4. g. 5. e. 6. h. 7. d. 8. c. **B.** 1. bike 2. exam **page 49: A.** 1. zoo 2. mitt 3. exam 4. math 5. bike 6. lab 7. sub 8. hippo 9. bus 10. auto **B.** 1. hippo 2. bus 3. exam 4. subtraction **page 50:** Possible answers: 1. wheel, fare, seat

2. wheel, handlebar, seat, pedal
3. scientist, experiment, measure
4. tiger, hippo, elephant, monkey
5. measure, add, divide, exam
6. ball, catch, leather 7. seat, head-
light, leather, seatbelt 8. engine,
fish, sea

Lesson 16, page 51: A. 1. cub
2. calf 3. piglet 4. foal 5. kit 6. kid
B. 1. swan 2. deer 3. goose 4. kangaroo **page 52: A.** 1. cygnet 2. fawn
3. calf 4. kit 5. piglet 6. cub 7. foal
8. kid **B.** 1. calf 2. cygnet 3. foal
4. kid 5. joey 6. gosling **page 53:**
1. cub 2. cygnet 3. foal 4. fawn
5. kit 6. kid 7. piglet 8. calf 9. joey
10. gosling

Lesson 17, page 54: A. 1. kayak
2. freighter 3. galley 4. marina
5. helm 6. mast 7. deck 8. keel
B. 1. pier, dock 2. casing, shell
page 55: A. 1. marina 2. kayak
3. galley 4. helm 5. hull 6. keel
7. mast 8. wharf 9. freighter
10. deck **B.** 1. galley 2. steering
3. kayak 4.mast 5. deck **page 56:**
Kinds: kayak, freighter; Parts: hull,
mast, galley, helm, keel, deck;
Places: wharf, marina

Lesson 18, page 57: A. 1. agree,
accord 2. sail, cruise 3. alter, change
4. steady, unchanging 5. improve,
correct **B.** 1. naval 2. formula
3. navy 4. format **page 58:**
A. 1. reform 2. uniform 3. navy
4. formula 5. navigate 6. format
7. transform 8. naval 9. conform
10. navigable **B.** 1. uniform
2. accept 3. formula 4. navy
page 59: Across: 1. naval 2. navy
6. transform 7. reform 8. navigable

9. format; Down:1. navigate
3. conform 4. formula 5. uniform
Lesson 18, page 60: A. 1. crash
2. rattle 3. sizzle 4. boom 5. bleat
6. purr 7. murmur 8. hum **B.** 1. bike
chain 2. doorbell **page 61:**
A. 1. crash 2. rattle 3. buzz 4. hum
5. sizzle 6. purr 7. clank 8. boom
B. 1. crash 2. rattle 3. boom 4. radiator 5. sheep 6. murmur **page 62:**
1. boom 2. buzz 3. rattle 4. hum
5. sizzle 6. purr 7 crash 8. clank
9. bleat 10. murmur

Lesson 19, page 63: A. 1. muscle
2. capital 3. palace 4. salt 5. vandal
B. 1. e. 2. d. 3. a.4. b. 5. c. **page 64:**
A. 1. teddy bear 2. watt 3. palace
4. salt 5. cereal 6. capital 7. atlas
8. muscles 9. vandal 10. ritzy
B. 1. teddy bear 2. Tallahassee, FL
3. palace 4. salt 5. hotel **page 65:**
Word chains will vary. Encourage
students to explain the relation-
ships between words.

Lesson 20, page 66: A. 1. review
2. subtotal 3. informal 4. unequal
5. misbehave 6. subtitle **B.** 1. Prefix
in- 2. Prefix *mis-* 3. Prefix *un-*
4. Prefix *re-* **page 67: A.** 1. misbehave 2. indirect 3. subtitle
4. unequal 5. recount 6. review
7. informal 8. unfold 9. subtotal
10. mistrust **B.** 1. sweatsuit
2. unequal 3. liar 4. letter **page 68:**
act up/misbehave, casual/informal,
not straight/indirect, suspect some-
one/mistrust, not equal/unequal, a
kind of heading/subtitle, another
look/review, not the final amount/
subtotal, a second count/recount,
spread out/unfold. The completed

picture shows a dog.
Lesson 22, page 69: A. 1. remember, recollect 2. retired, idle 3. hidden, unseen 4. show, reveal 5. lose,
mislay **B.** 1. Prefix *sub-* 2. Prefix
un- 3. Prefix *re-* 4. Prefix *mis-*
page 70: A. 1. renew 2. uneasy
3. submarine 4. recall 5. inactive
6. invisible 7. subnormal 8. misplace 9. uncover 10. mislead
B. 1. passport 2. ghost 3. submarine
4. trick **page 71:** Answers will vary.
Lesson 23, page 72: A. 1. darkness 2. catcher 3. forgiveness
4. rancher 5. distantly 6. government
B. 1. rapidly 2. amazement 3. plentiful 4. graceful **page 73:**
A. 1. plentiful 2. amazement
3. catcher 4. darkness 5. government 6. distantly 7. forgiveness
8. rancher 9. graceful 10. rapidly
B. 1. darkness 2. catcher 3. graceful
4. hare **page 74:** 1. plentiful
2. darkness 3. catcher 4. government 5. rancher 6. distantly
7. graceful 8. amazement 9. rapidly
10. forgiveness

Lesson 24, page 75: A. 1. fright-
ening, shocking 2. satisfaction,
pleasure 3. knowledge, mindfulness
4. teacher, instructor 5. newly, late-
ly 6.plan, agreement **B.** 1. Suffix *-ful*
2.Suffix *-ness* 3. Suffix *-er* 4. Suffix
-ly **page 76: A.** 1. contentment
2. Recently 3. tactful 4. frightful
5. performer 6. arrangement 7. quietly 8. trainer 9. laziness 10. awareness **B.** 1. performer 2. tiptoe
3. politeness 4. recently **page 77:**
Answers will vary.